Magnifyii g

Sue Finch

Enjoy!

Sue Finch

Black Eyes Publishing UK

Magnifying Glass

By Sue Finch
© Sue Finch, 2020

Published by Black Eyes Publishing UK, 2020
Brockworth, Gloucestershire, England
www.blackeyespublishinguk.co.uk

ISBN: 9781913195113

A CIP catalogue record for this title is available from the British Library.

Cover design: Jason Conway, cre8urbrand.
www.cre8urbrand.co.uk

Sue Finch's debut collection, *Magnifying Glass*, focuses the lens on moments in time and carries the reader from childhood through to adulthood. The title poem recalls one of her brother's experiments in the garden with his new magnifying glass and its ability to focus sunlight to make fire. The poems are at times dark (*Hare Mother* reflects on a woman leaving an abusive relationship), occasionally twisted (*The Red Shoes* is a fairy tale inspired poem that begins with a meeting in a shoe shop) and often poignant (*No Second Chance* recounts an autobiographical moment where poor use of an axe to chop wood has unforeseen consequences). The final poem, *Graphene*, is a love poem as well as a celebration of carbon atoms.

For the reader of fairy tales,
the boy with the magnifying glass
and all those on my poetry path.

Magnifying Glass

Contents

Descendant

I am descended from smugglers.
I hold the darkness of tunnels inside me;
hushed voices, past midnight, alert my ears.
I am descended from strong-armed men,
the readers of the sea.

I am descended from those who roam.
I hold the restlessness of wild words;
dawn hours tempt me with their offers of peace.
I am descended from storied women,
the tellers of old tales.

I am descended from the unknown.
I hold onto sunsets, dark dreams
and forests.
Reckless whispers ride my thoughts
the essence of my being.

I Can't Send You Back, Can I?

I

I can't send you back, can I?
she said.

What if I wanted to go?
To have her voice filtered through skin and fat.
Those words,
those questions,
that curious consoling babble.

What if I wanted to be enclosed again?
To be unseen,
hidden.

What if I wanted to keep her expectant?
To have us halted in anticipation.

II

Last time I led with my head;
tunnelling though grip after grip
of concentric circles.
A hot salted mucus sealed my squashed nose
denying me her scent.
Air on my hairless head shocked me
as my face squashed tighter
for my slow unscrewing.
The throb of heartbeats
confused me with her;
fast and faster

in my ears, my chest, my head.
Longing to cry,
my lungs had me impatient.
A metallic tang hung in shivers of cold
as at last my body slung out behind.
I was landed.

III

This time
I would be her contortionist daughter;
her womb my lockable box.
I would have to go backwards,
lead with my feet, point my toes.
Contoured contractions
would twist my legs into a rope
their powerful vacuum cramping, pulling,
spiralling me upwards
until the smooth, curled width of my hips
pushes her pelvis, demanding to come in.
My left shoulder would force her wide
just before that warmth grabs my neck.
Her stretch for the sharp shock of my head
would finally close my eyes.

Flamingo
after Liz Berry

The night she bent my elbows
to fit the candy floss cardigan
for the twenty-third time, my limbs turned to wings.
She wished me to be a pink girl.

My neck grew and grew,
elongating, extending,
black eyes shrunk in the pink like submerged pea shingle.

Light in my fan of feathers,
I was lifted like a balloon puffed with helium.
Body and wings held stately,
magically anchored by one leg,
miniature rough patellas marked my hinges.

When the scent entered half-moon holes in my new beak
I could have salivated at the raw rip of scaled flesh
but my juices would not run – I was gizzard now.
I couldn't bear the confinement of the flock but flight
had me fearful.

Passing through flamingo phase I fattened, darkened.
A birch broom in a fit.
I shook my thick cheeks side to side
became a dodo
with a waddle in my walk that slowed.

She sent my father then. He came alone
with gun and incongruent grin
and shot me dead.

Skewered me above his heaped fire under moonlight,
turned me slowly round and round.

When he turned for the sauce
I dropped;
charcoaled feathers, beak tinged with soot,
burning in the blaze.
I laughed as I rose
higher and higher;
a golden bird from the fire.

Caps in Her Gun

She has the smell of thin, brown leather
in her nose,

a print of softness on its tip
from kissing Orinoco's hat.

She has tucked up the toys in her bed,
wished herself a cowboy for the day.

Holster on, bandana tied, sheriff badge shining,
she stands tall, shoulders wide.

Caps in her gun,
ready to shoot.

While Missing You Today

While missing you today
I worked out the relationship
between cubed numbers
and the six times table again.

I remembered red candlewick bedspreads
faded to pink
the throaty laugh of a ginger-haired boy
a wanted poster for a wolf spider
and two fifty-pence coins
slid behind Granny Smith's glasses.

I found old words written on thin paper
that proved my memories.

Magnifying Glass

Making sure his head does not cast a shadow,
my brother orders me quiet.

Watch, he says,
he has been experimenting for days
with the magnifying glass they bought him.

Now he aims the sun's rays,
narrowing
intensifying
targeting.

His control is powerful.

Between the far away sky
and us on the ground
he is manipulating light, tightening it.

He burns ants,
trapped in dips in the wood,
setting charcoal circles side by side.

He starts then on newspaper;
the heat bites crescents in the edges
like a hot-jawed leafcutter ant.

Smoke rises, lifting its smell
just before orange tongues elongate
and lap.

Amazingly, it kites up, up,
over our fence into the sky.

I stand beside, yet, behind him,
staring up into the space that he loves
and I do not understand.

My Man in the Moon

Lying in bed
I picked at the anaglypta
jammed my fingernails with paper and paste.

Stroking the grainy grey-white surface
I remembered Sunday's porridge,
how its tempting smell had lied about the taste.
I got lost in the thought that milky oats could stick paper,
that husks could be the wallpaper's bumps.

Time passed in touching and picking.
I found friction.
Mesmerised by the heat,
I rubbed my fingertips hotter
as if it might smooth my prints.
I watched the crumb-like drop of disintegrating plaster.

Then a crescent was there
with a nose.
I smiled as I picked him out
my man in the moon.
I carved his shape with the lid of a blue biro
coloured him in with felt tip pens.

That night I slept facing the wall
ready to show my mum in the morning.

But night's darkness stole my colours
faded red to pink
turned black to tabby-brown.

Mum was sparse with words.
I looked through a film of tears,
saw his sinister grin.

His Gun
for the schoolboy who entered my office without really
announcing himself

He shoots.
She is falling,
staggering
clutching herself
her hip seems to disappear.
She stumbles, hits the floor, stills.

He watches,
so silent he stops the air from moving,
her closed eyes flicker to find him.
He searches his words,
they both stare at it hanging from his limp hand.

He meets her gaze, speaks –
It's just a banana, he tells her.

Stung

If it was a wasp
it stung once and fled,
if it was a bee
I didn't see it die.

I stood naked
gazing at a splinter;
a black spine centred in a pink circle.

I pushed my stomach out to watch what next,
alone and naked in a field I saw
it redden concentrically as I stared.

I held out my arms to the Summer air
let my lungs expel their cry.

Fish Dinner

At first
he's an extra branch on the log
eyes sung shut
by the water's repeating lullaby
his dream too good to break.

When his nostrils flick open
I think it is my scent
that has pressed the switch.
Flex of nose forces eyes forward
awake now and looking, he sees.

Grey sky darkens,
a man stands ready with a bucket of fish
bullets of rain wound the pool.

The glass is suddenly too thin.
I dread the teeth but do not move.

Other otters come to blur the picture
their sudden hunger
filling the space between him and me.

Tossed fish hold balletic body shapes in the air
before being rawly razored in the tightest of grips.

I see my mother
attacking dab fins in the kitchen,
1977, Silver Jubilee Year,
scissoring viciously,
dumping them in flour.

She will fry them fiercely
a few minutes on each side
while she thumps the lumps out of mashed potato.

Fish feast over, the otters plunge into the water.

The rain flattens my hair.

A Desk with Flowers

She could have thrown the water,
removed the flowers from the vase
and thrown the water.

She could have just thrown the flowers
she could have thrown all three.

Maybe she stopped at throwing words.

I told her the milk was warm,
it shouldn't have been warm from a bottle
only from an udder.

I didn't tell her it made me think of farmyards
and the need for wellies against
splash of liquid brown.

Thickened yellow cream
clinging to the silver tops I had to pierce
with my straw
made me want to cry.

And the head teacher sat behind a desk
with flowers on it, in an office.
I don't know if she stood up
when my mum left
or what she thought,
but I didn't drink milk at school again.

The Seventh Car will be His

Only when her brother came to kneel too
could she exhale the sigh that needed to escape
from the jail of her too-taut lungs.

It will be alright, he said, sparing her a glance.
Are you sure? she asked, not looking.
The seventh car will be his, he replied.

Silently she stared, watching all movement.

Next door's tatty tabby sat on the kerb
washing methodically behind his ears,
a crisp packet, encouraged by the wind
that brought the rain, turned a somersault
and she wondered if it felt its freedom.

Time had halted in their house since last night.

She knew she did not want to see the truth –
the truth was hanging in the garden shed
the dead rabbit waiting to be skinned
claret-red blood dropped from its nose
supposedly concealed by half a blanket.

Multiples of seven came and went.

They sat watching, waiting, not yet crying,
suspended like the lifeless hanging pet.

Hare Mother

Last year's snow
turned your hair pure white.

A winter of wild words:
bitch, trapped, wasted.

His sharp preying eyes had you hiding,
almost glad when he went on the prowl.

Cunning Arctic hare mother you dispersed your litter;
your fully-furred leverets took their scent beyond his range.

Now, new winter, he's still searching,
you still yourself – hope holds you frozen.

Yet he's watching you, waiting,
won't just let you go.

You tell yourself they don't need you.

Then you run.

Darkness Fixes Your Thoughts

You have one match
in one small matchbox;
a patch of friction
still strikeable.

And tonight you will strike it,
for the spark tinged with sulphur
for the tiny erupting fizz
for the blackened, skull-hollowed match-head.

It will catch, everything will catch
hotter than you dreamed.

You will be grateful
for grey smoke invading your lungs.

You will not cough it out
the clouds it makes will be your sky
beyond them a hidden summer, kingfisher blue,
under which sleep will come.

My Dream Jaguar
after Pascale Petit

I bet you knew I was there
watching him watching me.
You bastard.

I was looking him in the eye
stilled by his open mouth taking in my scent,
tasting me.

Barefoot in his paced and sprayed territory
I listened to the seconds passing as I breathed.

Then you gave me that nightmare again –
you standing at the end of my bed,
your feet either side of mine
weighing me down
your arms out-stretched
like the crucified Christ from my *Children's Bible*.
Yet your eyes aren't jewelled blue
and you sneer
before letting yourself fall.

The weight of your body wakes me.

I want to be back, forehead to forehead,
breathing the warmed dust scent
on his burnt black fur.
I want him curled around me,
nesting me in his lap
as his gentle soporific breathing
sings to me.

I want warm fur
rising
falling
the lazy rumble of the purr in his chest.

I want two nonchalant licks on my cheek
from that rasped tongue that say,
wait there,
before his eyes flick to hunter
and he rises for you.

The Antiquarium

After lunch they often went to the antiquarian bookshop;
their every other day companionable walk.
Leaving behind the morning's Monopoly, Ludo, Chess
for old burgundy spines with gold lettering.
Time out in a place of possibilities
where grey dust got disturbed and
words were waiting to be seen.
He wanted old battles, dinosaurs, classified animals, God.

She was all table-tops not shelves.
On the horizontal, where books moved, dust didn't gather
pages were tatty from handling, not age.
Rapidly her sharp eyes swept and scanned
seeking out the sex while he was too absorbed to know.
She bought twenty pence orgasms that she did not know
were fictioned.

Phoning Richey Edwards

no landline, no mobile, the call was made from a phone box

Stagnant air moved as I entered
disturbing sour nicotine, old urine.

Dampened cigarette ends lay split open
orange tobacco strands twisting out
like untidy moustache hairs.

Pockets loaded with coins I was ready.
Above staleness another smell rose;
the shelved phonebook
its pages thumbed and flicked.

I was ringing to say *happy birthday,*
he was called to the phone
as if he might know who I was.

We spoke, but I can't recall the words.
I have an echo of a gentle lilt
that floats across my mind from time to time.

I called; we spoke.
I wish I had the words.

Rapunzel

Rapunzel: A fairy tale by the Brothers Grimm
rapunzel: lambs' lettuce (Campanula rapunculus)

Only ever iceberg now
and always from the fridge
I peel away the outer leaves;
two, three,
sometimes four have to go
before it is pale enough for my taste.
Then, eight wedges
crisply cut
are my bland supper.

Frigid, he says.
He does not know what it does to me
that you are not here to take the milk.
Salty tears trickle down my neck
souring the moisture
that leaks from my breasts
each time I shift in the chair.

I knitted you a purple blanket,
grew it each evening after dinner
twelve weeks of moss stitch
to wrap my precious baby.
I never got to see you in it.
He took you on the darkest night.
I hope he wrapped you well
kissed you
before he handed you over.

He should have gathered us both up, you and I,
run us far away
he should have built us a castle
of thickest stone,
moated us in.

I listen for you crying in the night,
think I hear you
as the clock strikes the even hours.

When at last I sleep, I see you.
There's the most magnificent tower
standing against the clearest blue sky.
The grey bricks are your dress,
sea glass glints and winks,
embedded in a mortar Empire line;
says you're beautiful now.
And there's your face at the highest window
smiling before your mouth opens.

I think you are going to call me mother
instead you sing
sending notes travelling
like unencumbered birds soaring.

I listen for you crying in the night,
think I hear you
but I don't
because I swapped you for lettuce.
And he let me.

The Red Shoes

Never danced with a boy
wanted to
couldn't flirt and risk the invitation.
No rhythm. No chance.
I imagined the red shoes would do the trick.
Too impatient to save (twelve weeks an eternity to me)
I distracted him; the Saturday boy
whose hands fumbled for bags,
whose fingers mishit the keys of the cash register.
He struggled to fetch the next pair
and the next
as I feigned tightness in the width
a squashed left little toe
my desire for a heel
a want for a bow.
The scarlet pair hugged my feet.
I felt the urge to stand and jig
my stomach flipped, I had to swallow a smile
I like these, I told him. *But wonder*
would black be more appropriate?
He withheld a sigh and readied himself for the ladder.
Top shelf, he mumbled as he stood to fetch them.
Halfway up the ladder
I laughed and left.
Had to grip my belly to hold myself together
as the chuckles came and came.
My feet spent their energy;
a jig, a reel, a reel, a jig.
I danced smiling at my new beat.
I roared as I polkaed –

my lungs grabbed for air
reeling, reeling,
I could not find the oxygen within my breaths.

The woodcutter smiled to see me
leaned back to enjoy the one woman show.
No, no, no! I panted in horror. *It's the shoes!*
He stepped behind me
resorting to an imitation of my steps to keep time.
I wanted to laugh at the big booted feet dancing with me;
cartooning each step,
caring enough not to step on the hated shoes.
I could only weep.
He held me.
I trembled the rhythm of my legs
offered him one foot, one shoe.
He gripped,
yet his giant hands could not master the vice-like leather
he pushed my shoulders away in horror.
I danced to his axe
shocked him sick when I struck:
one foot, two feet
no feet.

Rumplestiltskin

I've had her necklace
and I've had her ring.
Her baby is next –
I'm Rumplestiltskin!

Midnight, mid-forest
the strange little man
grinning and singing,
dancing and spinning.

His voice rising like the grey wood smoke
higher and higher
wisping up and away as
stilled and silent I watched.
I swear I saw notes in the air!

No slowing at all
he danced on and on,
no notice he paid me
then I was gone
back to the room of gold
where you, my baby, my precious, slept.

For hours in days I had been tormented
while you breastfed, I had guessed and guessed again
added to my list all the time you slept.
Started with 'Muttonchops' and 'Lacedleg',
used nicknames, pet names, biblical names.

Then in desperation I changed his gender:
Amelia, Felicity, Belinda.

When next he arrived whirling, I would win
he would not be my baby thief.
I held you to me and wept, relieved.

Sir Still Unkempt you are!
I told him when he came.
I think I am ready now
I   shall   guess   your   name...
Are you Stinkerlumplist?
Plunkerslimtits?
Trinketslumlips?
        Tinklerumsplit?
(With each name I said he became more red.)
I know you now Rumplestiltskin,
you strange and funny little man.
Harassed, embarrassed
he stomped and swore:
a titanic tantrum.
The ground creaked and cracked
and down he went.

A shout echoed:
I hate you!   I hate you!
Hate you!

Then he took in each hand
his curly-toed shoes
and tore himself
quite neatly in two.

Fe, Fi, Fo, Fum

Today I mopped the kitchen floor
while doctors opened your right leg
to put titanium inside,
to take away the grinding bone.

I'll grind your bones to make my bread!
There's your deep, pretend giant's voice.
I am five years old
I am seeing the pictures in my head as you read.
I am looking at you,
the light in your eyes offsets the threat,
your arched eyebrows hold Jack and giant apart
you keep Jack ahead all the way down.

The axe, mother! He calls.
I fear she is busy and will not come
she has hardly noticed her child is gone
yet you have her running
brandishing the tool
saving the day.

The floor dries. I drink tea.
I shudder at the thought of your bones
in the incinerator.

Siren Song of My Mother

The siren song of my mother calls me;
her long notes pierce the unfocused night.
I am weighted, but pulled towards the sea.
Slices of waves, jewelled under lunar light,
shine, before clouds shroud her as I begin to swim.
Riding the waves, the music brings calm
I want to sit with her, limb touching limb,
as sea salt stiffens the hairs on my arms.

Separated by birth and then by time
I need her to encircle my whole being.
I want to know that I was hers and she was mine,
yet the song that she keeps on singing
is all melody and vowels now, no words.
I see only sharp shadow rocks, not her.

Apple Crumble

She taught you not to be scared of maggots
or softening brown bruises dotted with mould,
together you chopped green-white apple chunks
on thick wooden boards,
watched scales gently tipping to accuracy.
She put the smell of rubbing-in
in your memory.

She taught you patience
as together you waited for juices to bubble
sugar to melt
edges to brown.
You learned the joy of anticipation
when you both loaded your spoons
with claggy crumble coated in custard
and, smiling, paused
before the eating began.

And now you dream
of portioning her ashes,
spooning them into matchboxes
ready to sprinkle her on the beach at low tide,
under lavender bushes in the park,
amongst the bread thrown for birds.

You wake crying at the thought of
strange grey lily-pads on the pond.

Blue Flamingo

Himalayan poppies flower just once and then die.
These vibrant 'blue poppies' have large saucer-shaped flowers.

One hundred Himalayan poppies
began with the chilling of a bone china saucer.
I sowed the seeds in rows on damp paper towel
summoned patience.
Four weeks in my three-degree fridge
to break the slumber spell.

Then I laid them lightly on soil
in pots, in the parlour
watched them daily, for root and shoot
waiting at eighteen degrees
until they were dormant no longer.

I wanted to change you;
make you paradeable, enviable.
I needed you to turn heads
forgetting that you once turned mine.

I fed them rich fertiliser
hardly minding that it clung to my fingerprints.

Lime-green buds fattened shyly
lips closed over a secret
until crinkled petals,
the blue of early morning summer skies,
broke through.

I ground lapis lazuli
pounding my pestle and mortar

dropped each flower into a barrel
sprinkled in the powdered essence.
And later, when the sun had set,
I mashed hard herring roes with all that blue,
slept while it steeped.

It was a Sunday at dawn I first sprinkled it in your pool.
You beaked it greedily.

I waited for your fledgling colour,
that smudged white,
to be overtaken by the shade I had chosen.
I smiled when I saw what I had done.

As if to mark your newness,
that blueness,
a pair of kingfishers darted past.

Sensing the celebration
you footed the ground then ran
in that stumbling way of yours
before parading your sapphire span.

Your Pinks Match from Head to Toe

It leaves me speechless –
though you wear it so often,
or at least every other Wednesday.

I have to stare
to check that the pink wooden hoops
in your ears
match
the pink, plastic belt
round your middle

that the pink shoes
with pink heels
match
the colour on your lips
match the stripes on your shirt.

Then back to the lips
that are forming words,
you smile
I am caught
your eyebrows rise encouragingly.

No Second Chance

The winter had brought me darkness,
made me cold to the bones
kept me hidden inside.

A need for warmth set my desire for kindling.

A wigwam of newspaper and dried twigs
waited in the grate.

And there was the axe,
weapon-ready from the night before
when I feared an intruder in the cellar.

I swung and missed first time.
The log wobbled,
rocked before settling,
like the last vibrations of a saucepan lid
dropped on the kitchen floor.

So, I held it still;
thick log suddenly dainty
between my thumb and forefinger.

Next swing hit.
Metal threatening my veins
with black paint and mud.
I needed to bleed.

The air, fresh with evergreens
and lingering frost
held my mind sharp.

I couldn't look.
I just raised my hand
as if to ask a question
and began pacing.

Wash it under the tap, she said.
Too fragile, hardly joined,
I refused.

I saved my fainting for the doctor,
for the moment he wielded metal trimmers
to scissor my finger straight.

Predators

We wait for hours that afternoon, watching.
Pretend predators, crouched and still
with the softest of breathing.

I had once glimpsed inside the mole-man's coat
where pinned moles hung
like counterfeit goods for the buying.
I shook my head at his cold calling on my doorstep
careful not to wrinkle my nose at his horsey smell.

Making tremors of the crumbly pile,
our live one loosens the earth,
twice its fleshy nose shows itself
as its pinkness breaks through
I stare at the snout as it sniffs.

Tiny wrinkles crinkled it on the outside
inside it was a raw, redder pink. I recoil.

Slit-like eyes come after
then clawed paws; over-proportioned shovels.

As I jigsaw the creature together in my mind
you reach a gloved hand in.
Thoughts of your destroyed lawn tighten your fist.

He only wants a few cubic centimetres of air
and now is surrounded.

His black fur loveable

a velvet that would have been strokable
had it not been peppered with grains of sandy soil.

You place him in the laundry basket
and we survey our catch.
He lies still, waiting for us to decide.

You can't hurt him, I say
and you nod,
perhaps wondering if he was loved underground.

You walk him four furlongs
before setting him free.

That Pigeon

You scrunched the bag like a gleeful child.
Don't! I warned,
worried that even a small offering of crisps
would activate every pigeon's radar.
You pointed to the toeless foot,
I shivered at the fleshy pink stump tinged with grey,
were you really showing empathy for a pigeon?
Poor crippled pigeon, I laughed as it pecked gratefully.
You were engrossed,
your eyes had not focussed on me like that for months.

Leafcutter Ants

Bold green flags held high
determined lines make their processions.

You watch for a while
then tell me they are repetitive.

Out and back again
building underground fungus farms
to feed foragers, strengthen soldiers,
keep the workers working.

So, it's out and back again,
out and back again, you say,
food, work, fight, sleep,
some sex –
just an endless cycle.

With a purpose, I tell you,
each playing their role
all bow down for the queen
fight for her protection
her death will be their doom.
If she dies, they die.

But they're going to die anyway,
you say.

Reading the Rules

I mark my quadrant,
liking the grass within my random square
regular grass, not lime nor forest green
30cm by 30cm
not imperial.

I keep the surface quiet
I do not have the patience
for tap, tap, tapping
like the hardly weighted blackbird.
My method: watery washing up liquid
lightly sprayed, watch and wait.
No sign.
Minutes hurt my legs.
I strengthen my mix.
Then they come;
countable worms for me to collect.

But things aren't right
thirty minutes has my five worms writhing.
They are dying.

With her I could not wait,
thought that kiss meant we were lovers,
moved my life north-west
exaggerated love and sex.

Years later I read the rules:
even plain water is a stimulant
vibrations only are to be used

charmed worms are to be released
after the birds have gone to roost.

My Bread Museum

At breakfast on the penultimate day
I used the sleeve of my freshly pressed shirt
to smuggle a white roll from the buffet;
so pale, so very soft like your cheeks.

I centred it in my case on unworn socks.

Retrieving it after a long, long flight
I grinned, relieved that it was still intact
and set it on my windowsill to dry.

You tried to throw my souvenir away
told me it was useless and unfunny.

Watching it harden, I wished that I would.

Long after the removal van you hired
had gone, I still kept it.

New windowsill, old exhibit.

Dusting my strange ornament made me smile.
I added to it often…
wheat freckled, wholemeal baguette
mini white cottage loaf
rosemary and potato ciabatta
a slice of 'one-night stand' extra thick white;
steadily building my bread museum.

Darling

A wide word
invented for those who can't remember
the names of lovers.

It echoes in hallways
on the edge of bedtime
as cars pull out of driveways
at supermarket tills.

It can be delivered in moments of potential
when sweat is made
or tea.

Sometimes it parades in full red roses
bounces like summer breasts
pouts and flirts.

Sometimes it simply offers a hug
or says it's sorry.

A wide word
that slips out on a breath
and pulls someone in.

Do Not Coffin Me

Lay me on a wooden platform
flat on my back
let my hands be gently clasped.
Rough and ready planks are fine
as long as they are splinter free.

Do not coffin me.

Set me on rollers so I'll glide
with the slightest push,
kiss the pads of your fingertips.
Set me off with this touch
and remember how much we loved.

Do not coffin me.

You do not need to screen the flames,
feet first I'll take the force of their heat
to set me sitting.
Let me ride the ultimate ghost train
facing my shadowless future.

Do not coffin me.

Burn me to ashes
make me weightless and free.
Do not send me down
where flesh swells and rats argue over eyes
I do not want to be a feast for worms that suck.

Do not coffin me.

Once I am gone make it quick,
send out a prayer for what I was
let me be light so I am in the air.
Wait for me to float
in and out of your memory.

Sloth

Looking up she points you out;
an untidy ball
suspended by overlong claws
that I swear are made from mahogany.

Hooked we stare.

We think we see you move
but it is the dizziness in our blood
from craning necks, refocusing eyes,
that twitches, not you.

We are willing you to flex;
you, our shooting star in hypnotic sky,
we do not dare to blink.

Yet your face stays
nestled in bed-headed fur
your hot breath clouds around your nose
moistening the dusty twigs caught in your coat
with the hay-like scent of eaten leaves.

You are brewing
an intoxicating sleeping potion.

We too will slow
if we stay and watch.

A damp green smell rises from the terrapin pool.
Remembering algae can grow on you
I turn to leave.

The Hanged Man

You have hung yourself
in the bare branches of a winter tree.

At first, I think you positioned yourself there so
my headlights would find you,
lighting you from the dirty, grey morning
pulling my head your way
warning me
daring me to focus.

As I get closer, I realise that your eyes will be revealed
and there's nothing I can do.
Can't slam the car into reverse;
I'd have to brake first
then I'd be right alongside you
having to look
and I fear it's only you and me on this street.

My eyes are drawn upwards.
I see you,
you meet my stare
my lungs are frozen

until I see a tattered bag in a tree.
The wind fills your head
escapes from the eye holes
rubbed through long ago by pavements,
rocks and fences.

Battered branches with no hint of green
are your long arms

the trunk is your tallness
the streetlamp your gallows.

Not Impossible

She waits for the oil to heat

believes she can make it for you

the real waxed moon
with all its craters and shadows.

She wants to plate that poppadom moon

will watch you crack it.

Do Horses Cry?

I make the promise
to leave work early.
I break it.
The clock takes me past seven
time and again.
You fill time without me.

Standing, bag packed,
tired eyes checking:
sockets off, laptop closed.
I turn, at last, to the time
surprised to see 17:15.
I imagine your smile.

The roads are busier now
I remember this as I sit in a slowed line.
There are the horses
I always see the horses.
Today I am slow and they are still;
one stands unmoving
as the breeze lifts its mane
drops it
lifts it.
I see us letting the sand run through our fingers
on a summer beach.

One lies.
I do not believe it sleeps,
cannot convince myself it sleeps.
My mind rushes:
it is dead.

Frozen by grief
the other cannot move away.
Would there be tears if I was close enough to see?
I don't cry anymore.

When you die will I stand unmoving
a silent statue of my grief?
Will I remember the time
I drove home early
to make amends?

Walking to Moel Arthur

We packed the rucksack
with more than tissues and water
tied our boots, checked laces.

On the way up
we stopped looking at our watches
let time surround us.

But at lunchtime
I worried that if I sat down
I wouldn't get up;
where we were going seemed so far.

The sun diluted and dipping
threatened to leave our muscles cold.

We did not really speak
as we ate our separate lunches,
mine seemed bland and I didn't ask about yours.
I only sipped my water
as I studied the path ahead;
narrowing and bending
hiding its end.

I couldn't tell if we were halfway to our halfway.
I wanted to read your mind,
were you for giving up?

I wanted to ask you,
If we turn back, will we ever come here again?

No Rabbits in the Hours Before Dawn

Suddenly the whole world narrowed;
wheat fields and green forests dropped off the edge
leaving the straight grey road halved by white lines.
Ahead an unreachable horizon
no hills
and no rabbits in the hours before dawn.

My world became
a clouded midday of stolen shadows,
trees stripped of their leaves by Winter's return
offered their branches to ravens
who mocked with their rusty-hinge calls.

With that phone call I heard you might die.
We all will die, of course,
but we are not ready.

We have not seen enough
rabbits in the hours before dawn.

The Moon and You and Me

I didn't want to lasso it
or box it up.
I wanted to capture it for you.

A gift not wrapped
or tied with a ribbon.

But you were not there
and I did not hurry to you.

Instead I studied it
looked again in my rear-view mirror
to check I wasn't dreaming.

Intricately patterned,
a screen print mounted in the waking sky,
it amazed me.

I made a pact to take a photograph
or remember to take you by the hand
and show you when next it came.

I should have hurried,
uttered some words,
reached out
but I drove the planned, unchanging journey
in my own silence.

I slowed
as I realised
you had never forgotten.

It was etched in your heart
waxing and waning without me.

After the Concert

There will be songs
still singing in our heads
all the way home.
And later, when the whiskey's poured,
you'll say I drink your dad's favourite kind,
then smiling you'll tell me he would have liked me.
We'll sing our versions of what we heard
before letting the room settle back to quiet.

I will remember to un-silence myself;
remind you of that night
on the bridge in Chester.
Perhaps, tomorrow you will wake early
unweighted
for the first time in two years.

It is Not About Dawn

It is about that moment
before the dark time breaks,
being present in the silence
standing still in an exact moment.

It is all about when that first bird sings,
first light,
the fact that there is an order
that layer upon layer
sculpts the day's beginning.

It is about discovering how long it takes
before the crow starts to echo back
with his rough
cruck, cruck.

Llandudno Promenade One January Evening

Somewhere, miles away,
sand blows into drifts and ridges,
hot scalloped patterns
so dry.

Here on the grey width
it is rough balls of hail.
First, they fall in blurred lines
then they are dust
blown and brushed
by the rhythm of the wind.

Two lovers are kissing.
The hail is still hailing;
drenching the town
pock-marking the sea.

Rain-split rays
from a line of lamps
edge the dark promenade
where the air has echoed
so many times to…

that's the way to do it.

But here for a moment is a kiss.

Tender

I cannot yet kiss where it hurts.

Stitched to a pout
it will make a beautiful scar;
a smile tucked away under your left breast.

But now it is knotted.
Red.
Too tender.

Accept my tentative watch
over its raw line.

I eye its inches end to end,
looking for fade, for gentle blushing pink,
willing away shades of swelling and heat.

They have sealed you up.
Four neat ties.
Four spider knots.

Accept my tentative love
I am holding it tight.

She Came Late to Summer

She came late to summer,
had waited for a hand to fit hers
exactly.

Fingers linked to fingers
she was led
through dunes
across rippled sand to sea's edge.

There, as gently foamed waves breathed,
in, out, in –
sun-warmed shoulders
began their unstiffening.

The sun,
the salted water,
that mouth, those eyes,
had her barefoot
ankle deep
smiling.

Graphene

Perhaps, before their pencil, in that building
it was in me – that flat form carbon atom;
hexagonally honeycombed
undiscovered and waiting.

And before that, did it come from a star?
Maybe it was once inside you.
You are a study in graphene:
cleaved graphite, harder than diamond,
stronger than steel.
Exceptional.

Biography

Photo: Courtesy of Kath Andrews

Sue Finch was born in Kent in 1970 and grew up in Herne Bay. She studied for a B.Ed (Hons) at West Sussex Institute of Education. She has worked in Primary Education since 1993.

Studying for her Masters in Creative Writing with Manchester Metropolitan University gave her the opportunity to work with students and staff at the Writing School. This enabled this collection of work to become a book.

She lives in Flintshire with her wife and enjoys walking up and around Moel Famau, strolls around Chester Zoo and exploring the coast and countryside of Snowdonia.

Stories and poems were a key feature of Sue's childhood. Read to each evening by her mother before bed, she credits this with giving her a fascination for fairy tales and the lessons that can be learned from reading. When her mother said, *I don't know where you get your ideas from,* Sue was quick to credit her mother for the dedication to the comfort of bedtime stories, early library membership and the encouragement to escape into books and reemerge changed.

This enrichment of imagination gave Sue the inspiration to swirl words around and rearrange them until they say what she wants them to say. Reworking and redrafting poetry often involves Sue taking a poem for a walk or letting it rest during a night's sleep to return to in the morning. Sue takes pleasure in crafting a poem in this way and watching it evolve until it reaches a stopping point for her and can then be offered to her readers.

Acknowledgements

Some of these poems have appeared in published form:

'Graphene' was written for *A New Manchester Alphabet* (edited by Jean Sprackland) The Manchester Writing School, 2015.

'The Red Shoes', was published in *Ink Sweat and Tears*, December 2016.

'The Seventh Car Will Be His' was published in *Ink Sweat and Tears*, September 2017.

'Sloth' was chosen for inclusion in *Crossings Over* (edited by Ian Seed) University of Chester Press, 2017.

'The Week the Clocks Change' was written for *Humanity Hallows* Magazine Issue 6, June 2017.

'Llandudno Promenade One January Evening' was commended in *The Festival of Firsts Poetry Competition*, June 2018 and later pinned to the *Places of Poetry Map* in Summer 2019.

'I Can't Send You Back, Can I?' was published in *The Interpreter's House*, Issue 69 (the first online edition of this magazine), October 2018.

'His Gun' was published in *Ink Sweat and Tears*, December 2018.

'Rainbow' and 'Trawling on a Day's Leave, 1943' were pinned to the Places of Poetry Map in Summer 2019.

'The Antiquarium' was published in *Poetry Bus Magazine*, October 2019.

'Tender' was published in *The Interpreter's House*, Issue 73, February 2020.

'Walking to Moel Arthur' was published in *Dear Reader*, March 2020.

'Flamingo' achieved 2nd place in *Cheltenham Poetry Festival Competition*, 2020.

My thanks to the editors above who have published my poems – giving them a place in the world always made me do a happy poet dance. *Ink, Sweat and Tears* will always hold a special place in my heart for publishing the first of my fairy tale poems, 'The Red Shoes' – thank you Helen Ivory and Kate Birch.

Thanks also to all those on my poetry path who have listened to me, read and reread my work and encouraged me. I am immensely grateful to those of you who created poem videos for my '14 Lines' MA Project – you are all wonderful people.

This book has evolved because of the time and expertise of Georgi Gill, Josephine Lay, Peter Lay, Audrey McIlvain and Anna Saunders.

It has been cheered on endlessly by my beautiful wife.

Full Reviews from Back Cover

Sue Finch's poems are flesh on the skeletons of folktales. They are inhabited by creatures who breathe quietly in the human dusk. They are tender, straight-talking, yet can catch you off-guard with their slanted pathways.
Helen Ivory

Sue Finch is a writer of great versatility. Her wide repertoire includes poems that startle and shock with their strong themes (suicide, heartache, trauma within the family), and also quirkier, observational poems, poems which celebrate a star gazing brother, or try to bring the moon down from the sky for a lover.

What all her poems have in common however, is a charge and electric current, language that (in the words of Dylan Thomas) lifts off the page, vivid and immersive imagery and a rich musicality and a fresh new reading of fairytale and ancient tales.

To read Sue is to be transported to other worlds, not just the gorgeous yet unsettling lands of the Hare Mother, the Red Shoes or a traumatised Rapunzel, but to worlds in which the everyday is transformed into the stuff of myth and legend.

A glorious and transcendent read from a poet with a fiercely original vision of the world, and a strongly developed imagination.
Anna Saunders, Cheltenham Poetry Festival Founding Director.

'Sue Finch's poems have the ability both to beguile and shock you with their humour, tenderness and darkness. Her confident dexterity with language and voice scoops the reader up and deposits them firmly in the world of her poems, whether that be family history, domesticity or an old fairy tale seen through new eyes. Sue's writing is vivid; it's curious. Her poems question and challenge the reader to be curious too; it's a challenge well worth accepting.'
Georgi Gill, Editor, The Interpreter's House.